Log Spirit

Log Spirit

Linda Arms White

GIBBS·SMITH
P
PUBLISHER

Salt Lake City

To Robert Reamer, whose Old Faithful Inn taught me about spirited construction.

To Phil, Curt, Dan, Brian, and Warren, who helped me keep that spirit within today's building restraints.

To Trigg, who worked with me to make our own spirited house a reality—at last, to last.

Chair photo on page one © 2000 Roger Wade.
Photos used on pages 57, 18, and 75 courtesy Garland Homes, Victor, Montana; page 55 courtesy Timberlake Company, Kalispell, Montana; page 7 and top left back cover courtesy Montana Log Homes, Kalispell, Montana; page 39 courtesy Montana Log Homes, Kalispell, Montana, and Talbert Construction, Whitefish, Montana; page 61 courtesy Otwell Associates Architects, Prescott, Arizona, and Mary Margaret Interiors, Bigfork, Montana; pages 71, 57, 76, and 21 courtesy Lachance Builders, Whitefish, Montana; page 58 courtesy Snow Country Construction, Bigfork, Montana, and Montana Cottonwood, Joliet, Montana; page 86 courtesy JMR Interiors, Gates Mills, Ohio; page 85 courtesy Reichstetter Construction; page 82 courtesy Montana Cottonwood, Joliet, Montana.

First Edition

05 04 03 02 01 00   5 4 3 2 1

Text copyright © 2000 by Linda Arms White
Photograph copyrights as noted throughout

Published by
Gibbs Smith, Publisher
P.O. Box 667
Layton, Utah 84041

Edited by Suzanne Taylor
Designed by FORTHGEAR
Printed and bound in China

To order: (1-800) 748-5439
E-mail: info@gibbs-smith.com • Web site: www.gibbs-smith.com

Library of Congress Cataloging-in-Publication Data

White, Linda, 1948–
    Log spirit / Linda White.—1st ed.
        p. cm.
    ISBN 0-87905-925-7
    1. Log cabins—Design and construction. I. Title.

TH4840.W36 2000
690'.837—dc21   99-057471

Contents

Acknowledgments

In writing a book, while real life marches on, most writers find they need support from others. In this project, I have been fortunate to work with a patient and caring editor, Suzanne Taylor. To her and to the entire Gibbs Smith family, my sincere thanks. Robin and Kate, our daughters, have read and provided input whenever I could catch them. You are always appreciated. Thanks also to Brad, Sandy, Ryan, Amy, and Dennis for your love and ongoing interest. Fellow writer Nancy Phillips has tweaked grammar, corrected spelling, and fine-tuned sentences, often on short order. She also lent an ear when needed. Every writer should have such a friend. Your input is greatly valued. Special thanks to my mother, Miriam Arms, who can be counted on to be there when needed. My deepest gratitude always goes to my husband Trigg—partner in life, building, and book writing, without whom none would be so rich.

Linda White, 1999

Foreword

As a child, I moved with my family from Texas to Wyoming, where I became immediately intrigued with the low log buildings from the early part of the century. They spoke of strength, individuality, and determination.

In those early summers as we traveled, the day ended with a search for the right motel. My father never went to the office before driving around back. If it didn't match the front, he'd say, "Nope, that's a redo," and we'd drive on. However, he pulled right into cabins or motels made of log. They didn't require the same drive around the back. The message was clear to me—log is real and dependable. It's the same front or back, inside or out.

In the summer of 1959 our vacation took us to Yellowstone National Park. Old Faithful Inn was closed because of damage sustained in a recent earthquake, but my parents insisted we go inside. The repair workers were on their lunch break. The inn was empty, except for us, and cathedral quiet. Sunlight spilled through the windows, illuminating layer upon layer of balcony rails and supports. A bird flitted through the vast space. Since that day, only rustic architecture has interested me.

I knew then that, as an adult, I would live in a log cabin in the woods near a creek. I began dreaming of what the place would be like and eventually collected notebooks full of ideas.

Almost half a century later, my husband and I found the perfect property, and I finally designed that dream home.

Then, my dreams met reality. I found that many of those fine old details do not pass today's building codes. I also learned that the price of log homes has escalated, and building companies must keep on schedule to make their profit. As a result, many do not have the time to create imaginative details.

But with ingenuity, thought, and a lot of early planning, the natural rustic dream house can be achieved. This book brings rustic design and modern construction together. It provides information on understanding the possibilities and the limitations of building with natural elements and gives a broad view of building techniques that will allow the homeowner to communicate intelligibly with his or her contractor.

Details

Nowhere do the natural elements of rustic architecture come together more impressively than in the great hall of Yellowstone's Old Faithful Inn. The design, though monumental, is deceptively simple——a harmonious blend of a few natural materials.

As our lives become more crowded, busy, and stressful, we long for the peace nature gives us. When we need to get away, we take to the woods, staying in a cabin or lodge attuned to the elements and furnished only with necessities. It is there we find the solitude, peace of mind, and even strength to be ourselves. We return again and again, if only in our minds. Is it any wonder we want to take that feeling home to live in?

Now more people than ever are building homes in some form of rustic style, hoping to re-create the feeling of days spent in natural surroundings. Over the past few decades, thousands have tried to capture that essence by building log homes. Some have succeeded while many have not.

Today the skyrocketing price of such homes is taking them out of range for most people. In trying to stay within budget, many have settled for four straight log walls, a ridgepole, and a couple of purlins. Technically, homeowners have a log house, but the log spirit they were searching for is missing. It takes more than log walls to create that spirit.

What does it take? Coaxing those outside elements inside.

Some of the best examples are in and around the national parks. Old Faithful Inn, built in Yellowstone National Park in 1904, is the perfect example. The crown jewel of rustic construction, millions of visitors each year enter its big double front doors. Its details include a handmade wrought-iron door knocker and hinges, a massive central chimney, tiers of overhanging balconies connected by wide log staircases rimmed with

Straight posts take on the likeness of trees when curved-branch braces are added. Visitors who sit in this intimate curved-log-railed balcony at Old Faithful Inn enjoy a sheltered view. Beyond, ceiling framework and half-log sheathing can be seen.

Layers of half-log stairs railed with curved and twisted logs take visitors to balconies and rooms on upper floors of the Old Faithful Inn. Notice the ceiling finished with applied half-logs.

Logs minimally used create a rustic atmosphere no other material could match in this early view of Old Faithful Inn.

6495, Old Faithful Inn, Yellowstone Park.

gracefully curved rails and balustrades, and a ceiling seven stories above the floor sheathed in half logs.

The vast space is not overpowering. The combination of sheltered spaces next to soaring ones gives it a human scale. Continuity of design and material unites its elements. Prominently placed windows of various sizes and shapes provide views of the larger landscape beyond.

It is not likely that in 1904 the inn's architect imagined it would serve as many tourists from all corners of the globe as it does today. Yet, he provided quiet secluded spots on broad balconies inside and porches outside for escaping the crowd to gather one's thoughts or write a postcard.

You might be surprised to learn that most of those national park buildings, the ones we think of as log, do not have log walls at all. They are frame buildings with dramatic log details. Even Old Faithful Inn has few log walls. Because your eye is drawn to the forest of log railings, two-sided writing tables, and balconies, it doesn't notice that most of the structure is frame. It's not the log walls that draw people to Old Faithful Inn. It's the details, the ingenuity, and the strong sense of nature. These natural features feel solid, substantial, as though they have been there forever and always will be.

More than anything, such a building was created not just built. It grew from the eye of an artist and the hand of a craftsperson. Time was taken and care given to each detail. Whether cabin or castle, it is a work of art.

How do we capture that spirit for our own homes? The answer lies in the details—details carefully executed to replicate natural elements. By understanding and applying the elements in this book of details, any home—whether log or timber, ranch or high-rise—can have the essence of log spirit.

Stones and unpeeled log posts and beams straight from the forest forge a simple elegance to rival any medieval castle.

The low ceiling and the mighty posts offer shelter that is in direct contrast with the open sides and vast space.

A fishing bear is just as "at home" in this landscape as is the house. The use of several natural materials and many rooflines help the home blend into the surroundings.

Design

Log. Rustic. Lodge. Hear these words and images appear of sheltering beams, window seats near a stone fireplace, hand-crafted niches, shelves of books, and deep windowsills filled with potted geraniums.

You may know that in your future home you want a log-framed window from which to watch storms roll in, a huge stone fireplace by which to read a book, and a porch facing the sunset. That's a start, but many houses have some of those elements. The buildings that capture your imagination are more than some logs here and some stones there. It is not any one element that shapes that just-right atmosphere but all of them working together.

A combination of vertical and horizontal elements, variety of texture and material, balance of cozy and open spaces, and flow of space and cascade of levels brings a solid design. Without these, whether your project is small or large, natural elements won't bring it to life.

Nature itself was the model for the architects of rustic national park buildings. Those early designers wanted the interiors of their buildings to feel much like the outdoors. They created a room flow that follows the natural terrain with some rooms up a few steps and others down a bit. They were not necessarily square or rectangular but fit the shape of the land. Small, low-ceilinged areas for intimate times balance with more open airy spaces and slightly higher ceilings. No matter where you stood, you caught glimpses of other areas.

It sounds like the perfect place to live. The design "feels" right. The open, airy shelter is not confining. The variety of floor and ceiling heights is stimulating, and the glimpses into other areas add spaciousness and drama. These are the goals when using natural materials.

If you are designing a new home or remodeling an existing one, this is the time to re-evaluate a few things. Many personal requirements will impact the floor plan, such as family needs, budget, and the terrain and attributes of the chosen building site. Keep in mind how your family lives and what those needs dictate. Don't plan spaces for things you have outgrown or don't really need. Build for the people and activities that have real meaning to you. Clutter is at direct odds with natural features.

The home you are beginning should feed your spirit and enrich your soul. Spirited living is quiet, simple, minimal. Build only what you need, and build that with permanence and versatility in mind.

As you step into the design phase of your home, take your time. The hand-crafted details that will give your home character require thought. Before ground is broken, you must know exactly what each detail will look like, who will build it, and what it will cost. Once the building phase begins, making changes will be difficult. Each minute has a dollar amount attached to it, depending on how many people are standing around while you scratch your head.

Combining vertical and horizontal elements with a variety of textures and materials creates an exciting space.

You will want to take your project to an architect or log-home builder to draw the blueprints, but your home will be richer for your involvement, not only during the design phase but the entire process. You know your lifestyle requirements and the spirit you want. Knowing exactly what you want will increase the likelihood of getting it.

The following are general guidelines for log-spirit design.

Division of Space

Within the same square footage, fewer rooms with larger proportions will have better flow and versatility than many small, closed rooms.

In traditional homes, you will often find both a living room and a family room. But picture a parlor in a mountain lodge where one large room serves many purposes. There is usually an area with chairs and couches around the fireplace; a table for puzzles or cards; a comfortable reading chair or two; and a book-lined nook containing a desk and chair for writing. The living room of your new home could become a lodge room, comfortable for one, yet able to handle a crowd. Add an alcove fitted with a daybed and it can function as a guest room, too.

Look at rooms set aside for meals in the same way. Many homes have an eating area in the kitchen and a formal dining room. What if you combined the spaces allotted for the two areas into one and opened it to the kitchen? You'd open the plan to longer vistas, which makes the home seem larger and saves construction money by building fewer walls. If that open kitchen had a breakfast bar between it and the dining room, you could seat one or a crowd in comfort. If you attached the lodge room to the dining room and separated them with upright posts, you'd gain even more possibilities.

Does each child really need his or her own room? Siblings who grow up in a shared space often have a close-knit adult relationship. Your children might enjoy shared space in the rafters with nooks and private spaces created by narrow walls or closets around a central play area. For additional privacy, a section for boys could open off one side of the larger room while one for girls opens off another.

Once you determine the number of rooms, the layout will begin to evolve. Here again, you will rely heavily on what feels right. Most people want the kitchen near the driveway to facilitate the unloading of groceries. You will likely want to put the lodge room in the spot with the best view and bedrooms away from the approach and public side. Bathrooms will be in proximity to bedrooms, and one will need to be easily reached from the lodge room, kitchen, and dining room.

Versatility

A versatile room serves many purposes and will be comfortable for a few people as well as a large group.

For people—A room that is comfortable for a large group can feel cavernous when used by only one person. Solve this by including smaller places around the edges of the room. Simply arranging furniture in groupings can accomplish this. Dropping the ceiling in an area around the walls can add a new dimension, especially if furniture is placed or walls built to give a feeling of enclosure. These alcoves become cozy window seats, writing areas, or reading areas.

For many purposes—Design rooms or spaces that allow several different activities at one time. In a lodge room, there might be space for gathering with a few friends around a fireplace while others listen to music and still others play games. Think of the people who will use the room and their needs. During holidays, you may have three or more generations in your room. Imagine places for everyone to sit and something for them to do.

Perhaps you need space for one child to practice piano while someone else works at a computer. You may want a home office corner in the kitchen or dining room. How will the rooms be used? Which activities can coexist peacefully?

Hallways should be given careful consideration. In a spirited house, if they must exist, they are wide. Six feet is far preferable to the standard thiry-eight to forty inches. Lined with bookshelves and/or cabinets for storage, fitted with washer and dryer behind doors, tailored with filing cabinets and a built-in desk for

*Rich colors and textures combine
with a low ceiling to make a cozy
living space while windows open it to
the expanses beyond.*

household record keeping, wider hallways can become hardworking, functional areas rather than dark, narrow passageways.

Flow

The way in which rooms relate to each other impacts their versatility. If the lodge room and dining room are adjacent, their functions can flow into each other as needed. Few dining rooms could seat all the members of a family reunion, but with an open arrangement, grand-parents, cousins, aunts, and uncles can sit at the game table and additional tables can be set up in the lodge room without being removed from the festivities. After a meal, everyone can mingle in clusters throughout both rooms.

Glimpses into other areas of the home or outdoors help to create the feel of flow and spa-ciousness. When planning adjacent areas, think of the passageways and doorways as frames of the view beyond, and compose the picture in such a way that it is pleasing to the eye.

Room Shape

The alcoves that lend versatility also add texture and variety to a rectangular room. Variety of room shape and height adds drama and interest not available any other way.

You may consider building an octagonal lodge room or a round sitting area off a bedroom. Be aware: the cost of building is based not only on square footage but also on shape. While adding planes, angles, and curves increases interest, it also escalates costs of everything from the foundation up. Foundation forms attach easily

Two different rooflines add variety to a room where cooking, dining, and relaxing take place.

for a standard ninety-degree corner but require adaptation, adding labor and time, to shape other angles. In a log structure, any corner requiring shaped and fitted rounds of logs can add five to ten thousand dollars to your bill—that's per corner!

The price tag will decrease significantly if you substitute upright logs for courses of fitted logs and fill the spaces between not with log but with framed walls. When deciding where to keep logs and where to let them go, try to keep the logs in the ceiling. Nothing is more dramatic or gives a stronger sense of shelter and permanence than logs overhead.

Another approach might be to add a five-sided half-round to the long side of a rectangular room. (See floor plan, page 19.)

Scale and Proportion

Natural building materials have a massive scale and a visual weightiness that must be balanced by the scale and proportion of the surrounding elements. Scale defines the size of elements. The scale of a small Victorian sewing chair may make it appear to be a child's chair when put in a room dominated by the large scale of stones and timbers. Proportion is the balance of the scale of things that appear together in the same context, such as horizontal measurements to vertical ones. The horizontal and vertical elements, both influenced by the scale of building materials, must have a comfortable relationship. When using logs and stones, room proportions must be slightly larger than in a building with conventional materials. Visual weightiness can make average-sized rooms seem claustrophobic.

There are few rules to help guide you. A room too small or too short feels dark and claustrophobic. A room too large or too tall feels cold, exposed, and unwelcoming.

Try to envision your floor plan as the three-dimensional space it will become. Stake it out. Walk through it. Live in it. Understand its spaces, both vertical and horizontal.

While planning your home, keep notes on places you visit that feel right. You may find that those soaring heights found in many of today's homes, while beautiful, don't really feel embracing or comfortable. There is just too much space above your head, and the vertical dimension is out of proportion to the horizontal.

On the other hand, the standard eight-foot ceiling with log-supporting spans beneath it would feel like a cave. In rooms where you want to feel cozy, logs supporting the ceiling can begin around eight or nine feet above the floor. If your logs are twelve inches in diameter, your flat ceiling will begin a foot above the bottom of the logs at nine to ten feet. That does not feel oppressive in the average-sized room. The larger room, however, will appeal to the senses more if you raise the ceiling height or lower the floor level another six to twelve inches. Again, this is an opportunity for variety.

Where using a sloped or cathedral ceiling, be careful not to let the peak get too high. A rise of five or seven feet for every twelve feet is comfortable for most spaces. In areas where a steeper pitch is desired, consider breaking the vertical rise with a horizontal element such as a loft or landing to help keep the proportion within the human comfort range.

This great room's massive stone fireplace, log staircase, scissor-trussed ceiling, and flagstone-paved floor are reminiscent of old-lodge elements.

Siting

We've all seen those just-right houses. They catch us by surprise, blending as they do into their site so naturally, not too tall, not too wide, just right. What creates that feeling? For one thing, the variety of informal materials used in the exterior of the house. The design, usually asymmetrical, helps the home adapt to the natural terrain. Consider the landscape. Its profile has mountains, hills, trees, bushes, low plants, ground, riverbank, river. It starts high and steps, level after level, down and out.

The first thing that is obvious about a successful rustic building is that it blends into its surroundings. From the top of the structure, in any direction, there is a downward and outward movement—ridge, roof, porch, rail, planter, deck, landscape edge, lawn or natural grasses.

The height of a two-story building can be stepped down with roof slopes that extend the visual line down and out. Consider using landscape architecture, such as a stone-walled patio and barbecue along with plantings, to broaden the visual impact, bringing the vertical and horizontal lines into a more compatible relationship. The line of a long low home can be visually lifted to fit into its environment by the illusion of added height. Trees planted to make several height steps beyond the house will help balance the vertical and horizontal lines.

Walls

The mellow look of this room comes from the chinked, honey-colored, hand-peeled round logs, the light ceiling, and the well-spaced rafters.

Beyond being functional, walls can also be a palette for the creative builder. Finished walls will help define the approach to the home and will be a backdrop to the living that goes on inside. Wall structure will be one of the first decisions you make.

Walls shaped with natural materials offer a comfort that plywood, drywall, and laminate cannot match. Building with log walls has been the height of rustic construction for the past several decades, but as more families answer the call to live within walls of natural materials, fewer logs are available. The law of supply and demand dictates that the cost of each log will continue to climb.

The dwindling log supply is fostering changes in the building industry. Rustic homes are now more likely to use logs first on the details then on the walls if the budget allows. Log walls are being used in combination with others and the results can be stunning. If having log walls is important to you, yet the price is a stretch, consider doing the living core of the home with logs and using other wall types for the rest of the home.

Three basic types of wall structure are commonly found in rustic architecture—structural log, log or timber frame, and frame made of dimensional lumber with finish material applied.

Structural Log

Structural log walls consist of logs stacked in courses that join, usually by interlocking, at the corners. These log courses support the roof and transfer its weight to the foundation below. Variations in log-wall construction are broader than might first appear. Logs may be round or squared, peeled, skip-peeled or not peeled at all, milled, coped, chinked, and set together in any number of corner styles. Books on log construction will help you understand all of the choices, and each will impart a different spirit to your home.

Advantages

- Log walls follow the traditional rustic style. The massive appearance of log walls comes with an embracing warmth.
- Log walls have tremendous thermal storage capacity. As such, log-walled homes tend to be cooler in the summer and warmer in the winter than frame homes.
- Log walls first constructed on a log yard can go up rapidly on the owner's property. Once erected, logs form both the inside and outside walls.

Disadvantages

- Logs, even ones that have been dead a long time, continue to shrink, affecting the roof, windows, doors, fireplaces, interior walls, etc. Adjustments must be made for settling as shrinkage occurs.
- Since logs are porous, they can have problems with damp or dry rot, but most problems can be prevented with proper protection and care. If rot does take hold, it can be cut out and patched, or whole logs can be replaced.
- Careful planning is needed to provide spaces for wiring, plumbing, and heating. Most of these utilities must be carried through interior frame walls, behind baseboards, or between logs.
- The round profile of logs allows dust to collect and can force pictures to hang at odd angles.
- Log walls are expensive.
- Log interiors can be dark if not balanced with plenty of windows.

© 1999 Brad Simmons

Plaster or drywall add light, variety, and relief to log walls and provide a pleasant backdrop for the color and texture of furnishings.

Log or Timber Frame

Log or timber-frame walls are part of an entire building framework. This eons-old technique is also called post-and-beam, piece-on-piece, and short-log construction. It is often associated with barn building in this country, though it has been used in all manner of buildings throughout the world.

A series of upright, horizontal, and diagonal logs or timbers are notched, joined, and pegged or bolted together to form the frame for all walls and roofs. Smaller logs or timbers fitted to this frame provide bracing. To this structure, the roof, walls, and floors are affixed.

The bents, or voids framed by the framework, are non-load-bearing and can therefore be filled with any type of material presenting a rustic face. Choices include vertical or horizontal logs, cordwood, glass, and stone. If the area is framed with dimensional lumber, it may be covered with plaster, planks, shingles, half logs, slab wood, and board and batten. Lightweight panels consisting of rigid Styrofoam insulation sandwiched between two rigid façades are specially made for this purpose.

Advantages

- The framework of the finished building is highly visible and a treat to the eye.
- Some framing logs, such as the ridgepole and purlins, will be full length, but many members will fit along an eight-foot grid. These shorter logs are easier to transport, carry, and shape, requiring less machinery and fewer workers.
- Bents may be filled with two or three different materials—such as log, stone, and plaster—within one structure, providing visual relief and textural variety. Depending on how the framework and infill are dressed, the rustic mood can take on a medieval, gothic, or western tone.

Vertical logs support horizontal ones in this log-frame structure. Spaces between the upright logs, called bents, are filled with short logs and windows that invite in the landscape.

- No load-bearing interior walls are necessary, allowing an open, flowing space. Simple plank walls or curtains may separate spaces, making it possible to change the function of areas at will.
- Panels to fill the bents can be constructed on the ground or in a workshop.

Disadvantages

- Notching and fitting the many joints of a log frame is tedious and time consuming. Most builders construct hewn-log (timber) frames since round logs are more difficult to work with.
- Permanent posts in the interior can be troublesome when arranging furniture.
- Raising and pegging or bolting the prenotched, shaped, and fitted log frame can require heavy machinery and many hands. Installation of some bent-filling panels may also require the services of a crane.
- Bents must be well filled and sealed to prevent air and moisture leaks.
- Log-framed walls, unless the infill is solid log, do not benefit from the thermal storage capacity of log walls.
- As in log-walled homes, utilities must be carefully planned. Infill and logs must be drilled to carry wires and pipes without compromising the required support. Open spaces allow few hiding places.

Dimensional Frame

Dimensional frame walls are no different from those in most of the homes you pass on your daily travels—except in the way they are dressed. A frame of dimensional lumber (usually 2 x 4s or 2 x 6s) is constructed, utilities are run, insulation is installed, and it is faced with whatever vapor barriers are required, sheathing, and the desired finish. While most homes are finished with clapboard or vinyl siding, brick, and sometimes stucco, a spirited house wears something more closely related to the natural world.

Rocky Mountain stick architecture was built of frame and faced with unpeeled slab wood (the first slice off the log made by a lumber mill). Slabs were tapered, both in width and thickness. They were sold as firewood and could be bought for little cash. Artistic builders trimmed and affixed them to walls in interesting patterns. The form is being revived, and some half-million-dollar homes are sporting the look.

Stone can be applied to the dimensional frame wall. Worked with a rugged profile and topped with a log-style roof, stone walls proclaim solidity and elegant rusticity. Stone and log together might be the finest backdrop available for evergreens and geraniums.

Half logs can be attached to the sheathing with screws and then chinked. The result is a "wallpaper" difficult to distinguish from full-log structural walls.

A more rustic scale can be had by building the frame of 2 x 6s or 2 x 8s. While more expensive, if within your budget, these walls offer space for more insulation, deep windowsills for ferns and flowers, and a greater sense of timelessness.

Upright logs can be placed under the roof and ceiling logs, providing the look of structural support whether needed or not.

Advantages

- Frames built of dimensional lumber are the least expensive of the three types to build and can be accomplished by a determined owner-builder.
- Curves and angles are easy to achieve.
- Wiring and plumbing run easily through cavities within the framing.
- There is no settling inherent in the walls.
- These walls can be well insulated and tightly sealed using standard, readily available materials, resulting in a highly energy-efficient home.

Disadvantages

- Other than not being solid log (if that is what you want) there really aren't any. Just don't fall into the trap of using all standard materials in standard sizes. Nature does not come in standards and it can't be imitated without variety.

© 2000 Brad Simmons

© 1999 Brad Simmons

An elk bellows in front of a milled-log wall. In an existing home, you can achieve this look with milled-log siding.

Wall Materials

Structural log walls can be made of round logs, hewn logs, peeled logs, unpeeled logs, or skip-peeled logs installed vertically or horizontally.

Log or timber-frame walls employ the same materials as structural log walls, but you also need infill. The infill can be preformed insulated panels, cordwood, glass, or stone and mortar. Plaster, planks, shingles, half logs, slab wood, and board and batten may be applied to an insulated framework. All can be used on interior walls, as can wallboard, grass cloth, tile, and twigs applied in intricate designs.

Dimensional lumber frame walls can be faced with anything that presents a natural texture—stone and mortar, plaster, planks, shingles, half logs, slab wood, board and batten, wallboard, or grass cloth, as well as twigs applied in intricate designs. Textured paint blends with these natural materials and can be used where light or color is desired. In small amounts, copper and ceramic tile can add interest. Stay away from mirrored walls, wallpaper, and anything with an unnatural sheen.

When searching for materials, don't forget to watch newspaper classifieds in your area newspapers for interesting recycled possibilities. Search salvage stores, demolition sites, and secondhand stores.

This home is built with hand-hewn log walls. A similar effect could be obtained in an existing home by applying rough planks to the wall and chinking the spaces between. Note the delightful table built around the timber post.

Roof Systems

Whether simple or elaborate, a log roof system creates a mood of protection and haven that log walls are unable to provide. The design and budget for your home will dictate many of the decisions concerning the roof, whose design must be approved by a licensed engineer. In general, however, there are two basic types of roofs that can add that log feeling to your home:

- A frame roof built with dimensional lumber or manufactured, pre-engineered trusses with logs or half logs applied to the ceiling.
- A structural log system with built-up roof.

The **FRAME ROOF** is the standard type of roof construction for most homes today. A roof framed of dimensional lumber or manufactured trusses is the easiest and least expensive to construct. The roof's framework is perched on top of the walls, which form roof support and carry its load. This system may be made in a triangular formation, creating a flat ceiling for the rooms below and perhaps a bit of attic for storage, or in a sloped formation using scissored trusses for a cathedral ceiling. Trusses or framing members are spaced at distances determined by an engineer.

The down-facing portion of the roof system is paneled or finished with drywall to become the ceiling for the rooms below. A log look can be obtained by bolting full logs, half logs, or wood slabs onto the ceiling. Any applied wood must be bolted not only into the ceiling but also into

Meant to support horizontal log purlins, this log truss adds its own weighty statement to an open multi-purpose area.

35

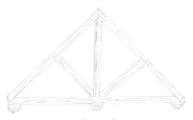

Framed-roof truss

Framed-scissor truss for a vaulted ceiling

the wooden framework. Care must be taken to provide adequate support for full or half logs along the bolt line within the framework. Ceilings in existing homes can be "naturalized" in this method.

Handling the framed ceiling this way is the least-expensive method to obtain the log look. The logs do not protrude to the outside, however, unless pockets are made for them within the walls. Logs could also be applied to the outside, as they are inside, to look structural. Either way, a skillful log worker or strong, meticulous home builder with equally strapping and precise helpers can achieve a look difficult to distinguish from structural logs.

The real advantage to frame roofs is seen when a complex roof is needed. It is difficult to fit logs to accommodate a variety of angles, valleys, and dormers; they are heavy and unforgiving. An experienced log builder is needed to make them work, and the price tag will correspond. When looking at a hip-roofed home, an octagonal roof, or a building with several different rooflines, the frame roof offers many advantages.

© 1999 Brad Simmons

36

The structural log system is built with full logs forming a framework that will hold up the roof and be visible inside the home. It consists of a ridgepole and either rafters or purlins and sometimes both.

RIDGE AND PURLIN—The ridgepole is the log spanning the horizontal distance from one gable peak to the other. The gable is the triangular area at the ends of the house formed by slopes of the two roof planes and the top of the walls. The gable itself can be built with log but is usually a framed wall. Purlins also span the gable-to-gable distance horizontally but farther down the roof slope. Purlins and ridgepoles must be large, long, very straight logs with minimal taper from butt to tip. These massive logs require support in the gables and usually within the house itself. This can be accomplished in the gables with log-gable walls, log posts, or heavy framing. Within the house, upright logs, heavy timbers, or posts hidden inside walls do the job.

In a home with an open floor plan or cathedral ceiling, a log truss is often used to provide beautiful support along the length of the purlins. A truss is a triangle of beams that forms a rigid framework. It becomes a point of interest and can and should be a work of art.

Purlins tend to give a contemporary feel to the building, as their size and weight kept them from being used in early construction.

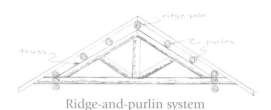

Ridge-and-purlin system

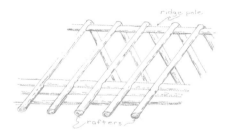

Ridge-and-rafter system

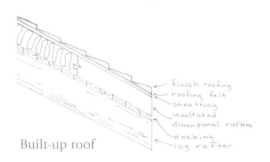

Built-up roof

They were not widely used until machinery was developed capable of lifting them. The advantage of this system is that fewer logs are needed to carry the roof load and give a massive structural feel. A small building sixteen feet across could require only two purlins and the ridgepole. Two purlins and a ridge means just six log ends to shape, resulting in a savings of time, labor, and resources over more elaborate systems.

RIDGE AND RAFTER—This system has the same ridgepole spanning the gables at the peak the previous system had but replaces the purlins with rafters. Rafters slope downward from the ridgepole and connect to it and the long walls of the home. Many more logs are needed with this system than with the ridge-and-purlin system, and each one must be fitted and notched. However, the logs are shorter, and therefore lighter weight and somewhat easier to handle. The downward direction of the logs offers an enveloping feeling that purlins just cannot deliver. In homes where the walls parallel to the ridge are far apart, rafters may be built over purlins to gain needed support.

Once the structural logwork is in place atop the walls, a built-up roof is added. A built-up roof is an entire roof built on top of the log rafters or purlins. It consists of a deck, insulated frame-rafter system, another deck, felt, and finish roofing.

The first layer is a deck that spans the logs. This deck must support the roof about to be built on top of it. Being structural it must be engineered and built of materials heavy enough to do the job required. Often 2 x 6-inch tongue-and-groove pine decking is called for. The deck gains strength not only from the thickness of the material but from the tongue-and-groove system that locks the pieces together.

On top of the decking a framework of dimensional lumber ten or twelve inches deep is built, with rafters running from walls to ridge. The cavities between the framing members are filled with insulation and vapor barrier, leaving an airflow channel above the vapor barrier from eave vent to ridge vent. Next come layers of plywood, of felt, and finally, the chosen roofing material. Yes, this is a Herculean roof. Its big advantage, other than the look, is in the amount of insulation it holds, which will be appreciated during the winter months.

Three courses of logs added above the first-story logs extend upstairs headroom while keeping the ceiling within the comfort level.

Besides structural support of the roof, other things will influence your choices.

COST—The simplest roof with slight slope, built of frame with logs applied is the least expensive to build. Of the structural built-up roofs, the ridge-and-purlin system is the most cost effective.

SLOPE—The slope is described as how many feet of vertical rise occur within a selected horizontal distance. Steeper slopes shed snow better than shallower slopes, making them desirable in areas of heavy snowfall. A shallower rise holds the snow on, creating an added layer of insulation. Many county building departments define a range of slopes that work well in the given locale.

Consider the effect the slope of the roof has on the interior of the home. The soaring spaces of a steeply sloped roof can be put to good use when combined with single or 1 1/2-story walls. By raising those side walls another three to five feet before raising the roof, additional usable space is gained for a second floor or open loft.

ROOF OVERHANG—Whatever type of roof you choose, a spirited house needs a heavy overhang. In addition to protecting your walls, providing shade for your windows, and sheltering the pup left outside when it

Upright logs, a log-lined ceiling, and expansive views give the feeling of sitting in a tree house. The level floor remains the needed constant as the rounded space joins the main house.

begins to rain, it is one of those things that sets rustic architecture apart. An overhang of two to four feet, depending on the scale of the rest of the building, will look great, function well, and help provide those shadows that are such an important part of rustic design. Before deciding the depth of the overhang, track the winter sun on your property. The same overhang that shades you in the summer will prevent the warm rays of winter sun from reaching you early in the day. Once again, strive for balance.

DORMERS— Added to a low roof where light and head room are needed, dormers should blend with the design of the rest of the roof and are typically either shed-roof dormers or gable dormers. Either can be framed in and dressed with logs. Shed-roof dormers in a ridge-and-rafter system can be had for little extra by simply raising the log rafters ends where they meet the wall so that they rest on a higher framework and shaping the ends to fit.

ROOF COVERING—Traditionally, shake roofs have covered rustic homes and buildings. In many mountain areas plagued by wildfires, the building code prohibits shake roofs. They are beautiful and authentic, but do you really want to top your dream home with kindling?

Fireproof roofing choices abound—roll roofing, composition roofing, metal, tile, cement, slate. Wood shakes treated with a chemical fire-retardant are a possibility in some areas.

Personal preference, building location, and budget will all play parts in your choice. However, pay special attention to the scale of the roofing material. The mass of stone and log require a larger scale or larger-looking material than does the traditional home.

Log rafters applied to a frame roof system carry the log theme overhead. Imagine the look of this room without the rafters.

A conventional composition roof will look shallow and thin. A spirited house wears a roof color and texture that blends comfortably with the surroundings. Many composition roofs today carry the subtle shading of slate. A green shade, the color of the surrounding foliage, could be the best choice for a home at one with its environment. Composition designs are available to give the impression of depth and density.

Roll roofing is an inexpensive and pleasing choice for a small retreat—not a large residence.

Metal roofs have a slick texture that can be jarring. Many different profiles are available, some of which help overcome this problem.

Tile, cement tile, and slate are aesthetically pleasing on log-style homes. The materials themselves are high priced and installation costs more than for other roofs.

Multiple roof lines are the hallmark of camps and lodges, with one roof flowing downward and spilling onto another, often of different style and slope. Varying rooflines connected to one another can be expensive in log construction, but with a little forethought the effect can be had without all the fitting. In the sketch on page 43, there are many rooflines but few intersect. The porch roof comes in well under the main roof, allowing sunlight into the upper story. The roof over the half-decagon connects not to the main roof but to the flat side wall under the gable.

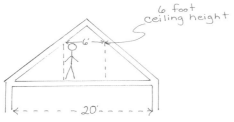

a) single-story loft headroom

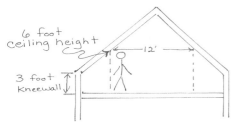

b) story-and-a-half loft headroom

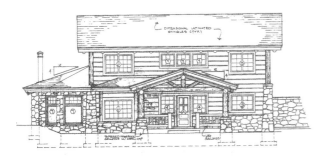

Roof Terms

Collar Purlin: The lowest roof purlin (horizontal beam) that sits on top of the long walls.

Collar Tie: Horizontal connector between a pair of rafters (one front, one back) that stabilizes the rafters and prevents spreading or sagging.

Common Rafters: Inclined roof members running from wall to ridge, closely and regularly spaced, that support the roof covering.

Dead Load: Weight of all the roofing materials (decking, dimensional rafters, felt, shingles, etc.).

Depth: Vertical thickness of any building material—log, timber, board, etc.

Dimensional Lumber: Planed lumber sold by lumber yards and lumber mills according to its dimensions—2 x 4s, 4 x 8s, etc.

Gable: A double-sloping roof that forms a triangle or A shape.

Joint: Connection point of two or more logs or timbers.

Knee Brace: A small log or timber that is framed diagonally between a post and a beam.

Live Load: The weight of the roof materials and everything it might possibly carry—snow, hail, repair workers.

Overhang: Projection of the eaves beyond the walls of the structure.

Post: Vertical or upright log or timber.

Purlin: Horizontal logs connecting gables.

Rafters: Inclined roof logs or timbers running from eaves to ridge at regular intervals that support the roof.

Ridgepole: A horizontal log at the roof peak that connects two gable peaks.

Shed Roof: A roof that slopes in only one direction.

Soffit: The part under the roof eaves.

Timber: A log that has been squared.

Truss: An assembly of logs or timbers that form a ridge framework.

Windows and Doors

Many people have stood on land preparing to build their dream home and staked out the house with sticks, rocks, and twine. With great ceremony, they have stepped through the "front door" to the inside and systematically looked out each of the "windows." On a spirited house, windows and doors help shape the atmosphere. They must be special, but that doesn't mean they must be expensive, just carefully thought-out and applied.

Windows

Windows open the home to landscape views, either natural or made to look that way. They break up the exterior house surface, adding life and intrigue. Windows must be positioned so they work for both interior and exterior design. The ones you choose will kindle a spirit and identity unique to your shelter.

There are many window possibilities. The floor plan itself will determine many of their sizes and locations, but if you are not careful, it is easy to be swept away and end up with a mismatched hodgepodge of windows. Use symmetry, alignment, and balance as starting points to assure a solid design. Then replace, add, or move windows to break up the staid pattern.

Window choices will be stock, custom, or hand-crafted. Stock materials are those that a building or window store might keep on hand, and they will be the core of the market—the most requested sizes and styles.

A simple handcrafted door combines with windows and forged-iron hardware for an unbeatable entry.

Dealers can often special-order custom sizes and shapes from the manufacturer. This might be one unique window for a special place to blend with a house full of stock windows or an entire house full of windows designed and built just for your project. Hand-crafted windows are available in some locations but usually require searching out the right craftsperson. Since energy efficiency is a big concern, windows may be the only feature in rustic building where factory-built models have the edge. Should you need a window of specific dimensions, a glass shop can install one without a finished frame. Once installed, you or your carpenter will finish it to blend with other windows.

Next you will choose the window material. You'll find all wood, all metal, and wood with the exterior of the window encased, or clad, in metal or vinyl. At first glance, it would seem the all-wood units work best in this type of home since wood is a natural material. However, one of the benefits of the rustic home is that it requires minimal upkeep. Wood windows, needing frequent painting or staining and oiling, don't fit that scheme. All-metal windows tend to have condensation problems, which can be a bane to the surrounding wood. They can also look too small in scale for a rustic house. Perhaps the best choice is the vinyl-clad wood-framed window. The exterior vinyl casing can be factory painted for a durable finish and the interior wood stained or painted to enhance the interior design. At the upper end, there are some fine copper-clad windows relatively new to the market. If within your budget, they look terrific with log and stone and will only improve with age.

Standard styles of windows are double-hung, casement, sliding, awning, and fixed. Function and personal preference are the deciding factors. Casements are hinged at one side and open on the other; double-hung are the traditional two frames that slide up and down; sliding windows slide side to side; awnings are hinged at the top and open at the bottom; and fixed glass does not open at all.

Double-hung windows flank a fixed-glass pane to form a bay. A window seat like this one built under a bay could become a favorite spot any time of day.

An entire wall of windows retains a sense of intimacy when framed with log grid work.

Fixed windows cost less than functioning units and can be used at a great savings where only light or view are desired, not ventilation. Pair a large fixed window with a working, grilled awning window above it for a lodge look. Use a bank of small windows rather than one large one, or even several layers of window banks, and frame them as one unit. Only one or two need to open. Set the grouping off with window boxes. A carefully thought-out marriage of clear glass and grilled glass captures the eye and enlivens the façade.

If you prefer a more contemporary rustic feel, use large windows with few or no grills. Remember, the nature of rustic construction is a balance of the cozy, open, and sheltering qualities. If "open" takes over, you have moved from rustic to contemporary architecture.

Windows in rustic homes often require larger frames than average. Use wider and thicker lumber, log slabs, or surround some with stone. Milled log siding can make a great door and window frame. The siding is milled when ordered from the lumberyard and is usually made with a tongue and groove. Request it be milled without the tongue and the groove or have your carpenter rip the tongue tabs off on a table saw and glue them into the grooves. The siding is available in four- and eight-inch widths. Occasionally six-inch material can be found. Choose window framing according to the scale of your home. Look at all door and window placements. Some may be up against an adjoining wall and not be able to handle wider material. If there are more than a few such places in which a different treatment must be cobbled

together, go with narrower trim for consistency. Whatever is chosen is part of a whole and must be continuous and congruous with the rest of the wood trim.

Homestead log cabins frequently had shutters. They were installed as often on the inside as on the outside. As areas became more settled and glass became more readily available, purely decorative shutters emerged. They draw attention to the windows and broaden their impact. Often they are simple two-plank shutters held together by a pair of horizontal braces with decorative cutouts. Pine trees, bears, maple leaves, tulips, and stars are among the many symbols cut on forest green, lodge brown, or turkey red painted

An octagonal window high in the gable adds welcome light to a cozy half-story bedroom.

boards. While shutters, working or merely decorative, are intrinsic to the cabin, lodge-style homes do not consistently have them. Often their windows are too large and the proportion of narrow shutters wouldn't work. On a weekend cabin, build some working shutters that close up the place when no one is there. Shutters don't always hang on the sides of the windows. They can also be hinged from the top and propped or secured open when not in use.

Doors

The same options exist for doors as for windows—stock, custom, hand-crafted. Rustic architecture cries out for wooden doors. Stock wooden doors can still be found, though more and more, stock doors are wood-grained fiberglass, vinyl, or metal. Buy the best quality you can afford, not only for good looks but for dependable service. Wooden doors can be given a coat of clear finish for a natural wood look, stained to match or blend with logs or other wood, or painted a rich color for an added accent.

Custom doors, usually an existing style in a certain size, can be ordered from some manufacturers. There are also door stores springing up that offer numerous styles and will construct whatever size and color you desire.

By far, the most desirable doors for rustic homes are the hand-crafted ones. The sky is the limit in both variety of design and price of hand-crafted doors. If the home you are building is large in scale, consider having your custom or hand-crafted doors built two inches wider than standard size. You'll find the proportion much more pleasing, and should you or anyone in your household ever need the use of a wheelchair, there will be fewer banged knuckles and door frames.

Doors can be found to fit any taste, including plank, traditional Z-braced, ones with frosted or stained glass,

Behind the forged-iron hinge straps and door latch lies a pioneer-style door. A similar one could be constructed by a handy homeowner.

and carved doors. The list could go on and on, but once you decide the type of door you are looking for, you'll be able to find the right craftsperson to build it. If you decide to take on the design and building or oversee the building of such a door, be aware that while everything you will see on the door—wood, design, door handles, and back plates—may be hand-crafted and possibly nonstandard, the knob and lock works (the part within the door) come only in standard sizes. Any door thicker than two and five-eighths inches will result in an adventurous search for a metal forger able to extend or build a working mechanism.

Recycled doors—from salvage yards, garage sales, demolition companies, or the want ads—are also an option, especially for the interior. Make sure they are not warped, and take precautions with old painted doors that may have been covered with lead-based paint. With doors or windows, make sure you obtain quality craftsmanship. You will use them daily, and those that don't work properly will give you years of headaches.

Porches

The porch is often an afterthought in modern house planning, but the rustic porch is an intrinsic part of the plan and should not be skimped upon. A well-planned porch can add another entire room of seasonal living—often the most relaxing one of the house. Porches are not only nostalgic but practical and unabashedly enjoyable.

There are many types of porches, and when choosing one you should evaluate appearance, lifestyle, and cost. A porch may be just big enough to hang a hammock or sit in a rocking chair with a bit of walking room left over for easy access to the door. Or it may wrap around three sides of the home and be destined to become the favorite gathering spot for family, friends, and neighborhood cats. Porches may hunker under the extended main roof of the house either under the eaves or the gable. More often, the porch has its own roof, setting it off as an architectural feature. It may be a shed roof or gable roof, or a combination of styles as with shed roofs running along the front and one side of the home intersecting at an octagonal, gazebo-like area.

When planning your porch, look at what you want to do there and what you need the porch to do for you. Probably first and foremost is protection from the elements. In a rainy locale with prevailing winds from the north, a shallow porch built on the north side of the home might be little used. The wind-driven rain will be forced to the back of the outdoor living area, leaving no sheltered sitting spot. The same porch on the south side, however, will be shielded from the rain by the house itself, stretching its livability.

An inviting screened porch could be turned into a year-round retreat by installing glass panels.

53

Houses often have several porches—the entry porch, the living porch, and the utility porch—each serving a different purpose.

The entry porch is the portal to the home. Its public face is generally a prominent architectural feature. A generous entry porch is one that welcomes family and guests. An ample roof allows several people to wait under its protection. A stone ledge or wooden shelf stands ready to hold mail or groceries. A protected bench has been placed where one can sit to wait for a ride, take off wet boots, or admire the sunset. It's also large enough to hold a jack-o'-lantern or other seasonal decor. Attractive and adequate light illuminates the door, the lock, steps, and the faces of those who come to the door. The door is unique to the building and a joy to look upon. The larger entry porch often has comfortable chairs or a porch swing, allowing it to double as living space. A few massive log posts and a log truss can create an immediate rustic atmosphere, not only for the space under its roof but for the entire sweep of the house and its landscape. The same posts and truss are a common and useful tool for establishing a rustic flair on a conventionally built house.

Living porches are often found on the side or back of the house, away from public view. That's where you'll find a hammock and other lounge furniture, play space for children, storage space for muddy boots and recycling, cooking and eating areas, and places to take care of utilitarian chores such as washing the dog.

How do you live? What do you want room for? Do you want cooking space on the porch? Will there be a charcoal grill, a propane outdoor cooker, or even a stone barbecue built along one side? If so, you will also want an outdoor eating area and perhaps a storage cabinet for charcoal, cooking utensils, and picnic supplies. Build that cabinet under the kitchen window and the top can serve as a counter or buffet. Open the window to pass through relish plates, potato salad, and cold drinks. Top the cabinet with tile to accommodate hot dishes and set potted plants there when it's not doing kitchen duty.

A screened-in porch provides a peaceful spot for enjoying the outdoors.

A delightful porch like this, formed by a few posts and a truss, could be built onto an existing building to capture an immediate rustic ambiance.

If your porch will provide rainy-day or shaded sunny-day play space for children, plan an out-of-walkway play corner. Consider lining one area of the porch with a bench and eating counter facing out toward the yard for meals, kids' coloring, and plants.

Stretch the seasons with a ceiling fan to enhance light summer breezes and a portable radiant heater to take the chill off early spring and late fall weather. Stone fireplaces have also become popular. They'll quickly become the favorite gathering place after a day on the lake. If you already have a porch and want to add a fireplace, consider a free-standing unit that will add immediate warmth and focus to your porch. These come in a variety of sizes, shapes, and materials and burn wood, gas, or propane. Ask questions if installing one under a porch roof. Depending on size and fuel, it may require venting.

Utility porches, often connected to the kitchen or mud room, may have a shelf where one can pot some seedlings or set garden produce until it can be taken inside. The space under the shelf is a place for recycling bins. Can you use the ceiling for storage? It's a great place to store a canoe, small boat, or fishing rods.

Screened porches are welcome in buggy areas. Screen panels can be built to span the distance between log posts. Attach them to the upright posts on the porch side or hinge them at the top and swing them up to hook onto the ceiling when not needed. Clear plastic or tempered glass panels can be made the same way. Take the screens down in the cold months and replace with the glass units and you have a sunny space for winter days. While you are planning, take time to design a storage place on the porch for those panels. It's more likely they'll be used if they're handy. The storage place could be a cupboard between the windows, below the windows, or between the porch piers.

We tend to think of porches as a single story, but consider these other options:

- A two-story porch under a gable roof.
- A screened-in upstairs sleeping porch.
- A porch with a small study or bedroom in its attic that is connected to the second story.
- The same porch as above but with a lower level incorporating a covered entry or drive.
- A detached screened gazebo or pavilion with cooking, eating, and sitting areas.

A shed-roof porch flows into a gable-roofed area set at an angle.

Posts and Beams

Nothing adds drama to a rustic interior like log posts stretching from the floor to the ridge above and heavy beams supporting upper floors or lofts. They tie the space together and unify large spaces. There are two approaches to using these features in a rustic house. They can be designed and built as integral structural components actually supporting the upper floors and roof system, or they can be applied to conventionally constructed frame walls that bear the weight of the structure above.

Structural Post and Beam

Structural post-and-beam construction is the embodiment of natural building. Posts carry the weight of floors above and roof system components, especially the ridge. The advantage of using posts as load-bearing structures, in addition to visual excitement, is that they can be placed throughout a building without dividing the space. In conventional frame construction, upper floors and roof systems are supported with frame walls that are then paneled or sheathed with wallboard. But with post-and-beam, upper floors, lofts, and interior balconies can be built while maintaining openness in the lower floor.

While a post stands vertically and transfers the weight above to the foundation below, beams are horizontal members that carry floors and

Posts unite with branch rails to visually separate the living area from the entry.

© 1999 Brad Simmons

Heavy posts and beams add warmth and substantiality to an open loft.

ceilings. Conventional construction supports floor systems with closely spaced joists made from dimensional lumber, usually 2 x 10 inches, or engineered-joist systems. These are then decked over with plywood to create the floor surface and sheathed with wallboard underneath to create the ceiling below. The result is a flat, uninteresting ceiling underneath. Traditional log construction places sturdy logs for supporting second-story floors. They are decked above with 2 x 6 tongue-and-groove pine and left open to the rooms below. The log joists are usually supported by heavier beams that are carried by exterior walls or posts. While entire floor and roof systems can be built with log posts, beams, and floor joists, the cost can significantly exceed conventional construction techniques and materials. Lofts and interior balconies, however, offer great opportunities to apply traditional features to a limited area while still achieving excellent visual impact. These lofts can have floor systems of heavy joists and beams and can be supported from below with log or timber posts. Add a rustic log railing to such a loft and you have created additional living space that flows from a central living area or entryway, adds interest and drama, and creates the feeling of substance and solidity.

Another candidate for selective use of post-and-beam construction is the entry porch. The stand-alone nature of attached porches, along with their fairly simple structure, makes it possible to build them using a traditional technique. They integrate well with a conventionally constructed house as long as the house design and decoration maintain a rustic ambiance, and they can create a visual impact from the outside that extends far beyond the porch itself.

The effectiveness of log or timber posts and beams depends on their size. An engineer will specify the minimum size required for structural soundness, but that may not be enough to achieve the needed effect. Minimally sized log posts can add a bit of spirit to an otherwise contemporary design, but a natural house should have structural members that match the volume of space. To provide the proper proportions, posts and beams, especially if they tend to stand alone, should be about twelve to fourteen inches in diameter. A row of closely spaced log posts supporting the edge of a loft or a series of log floor joists can be smaller both from a visual and a structural perspective.

Log and stone pillars unite with beams to extend the living space beyond the adobe walls.

Round posts and square beams form the perfect backdrop for elegant dining. This effect could be simulated with applied materials in an existing room.

Using a log with some of the branches still attached can soften the harsh vertical and horizontal edges and give a whimsical effect. Consider this method to create a log arch to house a door. Since it does not have to be structural, it could be built into a frame wall.

Structural post-and-beam systems must be carefully designed by a licensed engineer in order to meet prevailing building codes and ensure that the system can properly support the building. All structural building materials must be graded to ensure that they actually have the strength expected by the engineer. Dimensional lumber is graded and stamped at the mill prior to shipment to a lumberyard. If you use logs as structural posts or beams, they will have to be graded by a certified wood products inspector. An experienced log builder will know how to contact the inspector in your area.

Applied Posts and Beams

Excellent effects can be achieved by applying posts and beams to conventionally constructed ceilings and walls. These are real logs or rough-sawn or hewn timbers that are bolted into conventional framing or truss ceiling systems. Round logs must be milled flat on one side to fit tightly against the frame wall or ceiling. When built and finished carefully, they can be nearly indistinguishable from structural members.

There are several reasons for a builder to consider this option. First is cost. Unlike true post-and-beam construction, applied logs or timbers do not have to meet structural engineering standards for size or grade, so they

may be somewhat less expensive. More significantly, less material is required. Rather than constructing a complete system to support a roof, porch, or balcony, the builder can pick the most striking features of the system and simulate them with applied logs.

The other reason for choosing this approach is that logs and timbers can be applied to existing frame structures. Using applied logs in a remodeling project can enhance the log spirit of an existing home. However, logs that are too small or too sparsely applied can look like a pathetic attempt at the real thing. If there's not enough budget to execute the feature well, the money is better applied elsewhere.

Posts, beams, and plaster can be applied for a rustic old-world ambiance as in this bedroom.

Stairs, Lofts, and Railings

Stairways are challenging, but, when viewed as an architectural asset rather than just a necessary utility, they can become rustic centerpieces. Let one fill the wall at the end of the dining room, or wrap around the walls of the entryway. Let it disappear behind a weighty stone chimney only to reappear on the other side where it connects to a low-ceilinged loft.

The first requirement is that the stairs match the scale of the house. A home with grand spacious rooms may call for two sets of staircases, each leading to a separate loft or hallway, while a cabin in the woods is more likely to have a minimal staircase with stairs and rails made of natural material.

A large home also offers more placement options. Stairs can be wider and incorporate landings and platforms. The steps can create a gracious curve and widen as they flow out into the living area below. It's easier to spend an extra 100 square feet on stairs when you're dealing with a 3,000-square-foot house than it is when you're trying to maximize the living space in a 900-square-foot cabin.

Large or small, there are some guiding principles that can be applied. Location, size, layout, and tread and railing material all play a part in creating stairways that are a part of the living area of the house, not just a tunnel from up to down.

Handcrafted staircases create a dramatic focal point in this Aspen, Colorado, residence.

65

Location is the first issue that must be confronted. The location must blend into the traffic patterns of the house, and it must start and end at points on each floor that are easily accessible to the primary living spaces.

Architects are very familiar with the building codes for stairway width, tread depth and height, and railing placement and size. They will know how many steps it takes to reach from one floor to the next, and they will have ideas on where to locate the stairway and where to incorporate platforms and winders, those wedge-shaped treads that turn corners, and platforms. But only you can determine the purpose of the stairway in your home, and that will drive many of these decisions. What do you want the area to look like? And what will the stairs lead to?

A spirited house strives to create spaces that relate to each other and flow together. Why spend thousands of dollars on a striking stone fireplace if you close it behind when you leave the living room? Why support the roof with a massive log ridge and hand-peeled purlins or rafters if you cannot see them from below? You must provide access but still find ways to open the upstairs to the downstairs and create a more unified living space for the family. Spirited homes use

A simple log rail encloses a loft, making a private refuge in the master bedroom.

open lofts and balconies, clerestories, and atrium-like entries to do this, so the stairway plays a very prominent role. It's not a passageway between separate areas; it is a link that connects related spaces together and creates a whole house. The stairway is a central feature, not something hidden in the hall. It becomes an extension of the entry itself or simply the part of the downstairs living area that flows into the upstairs loft.

Stairway design, then, becomes an exercise in trading floor space to achieve the desired effect while still leaving room to hang your coat when you enter the building. As mentioned earlier, this is easier in larger homes, but apply the same principle to the small cabin and you will reap benefits in livability and atmosphere.

Location drives the stairway layout. The simplest layout is a straight staircase with no turns, landing, or winders. Straight stairs use space efficiently, but they lack interest and contribute little. The other extreme is circular stairs. Also space efficient, they can be a striking architectural feature when placed in a showcase location. Unfortunately, they can also make you feel you need a parachute to make the descent.

The most useful stair layouts will have sections of straight stairs connected by short platforms and generous landings. Such stairs can be L-shaped to fit along two sides of the entry or U-shaped to wind around behind a stone chimney or just to create a more open vertical

Weathered and twisted branches team with log rails to frame the stairway and loft office. The motif is echoed on the double entry doors and antler lamps.

space in the form of a stairwell. Winders can replace landings to conserve floor space if needed but will sacrifice some of the grace.

No aspect of building is more regulated by building codes than the layout of stairways. The National Building Code specifies minimum width, tread depth and rise, the dimensions of landings and winders, the height and spacing of railings, the location of handrails, and the amount of headroom required above the steps. Your architect or builder will know them by rote and will quote them to you in answer to many of your specific questions regarding the stairs, but you will seldom find them unduly restrictive, and they result in a house that is both safe and gracious.

Once the stairway location and layout are established, you must decide what materials to use. The most prominent features are the treads and the railings. Both lend themselves to creative applications of natural materials.

In a log home, treads are often formed from half-log pieces that are bolted into notched log stringers. The result is an open stairway with an appealing log feel. Be aware, though, that dust sifts down from open treads onto whatever is below. Don't locate your favorite reading chair under open-tread stairs. Other alternatives include pieces of heavy timbers or slabs or blocks of stone. Either can easily be backed with risers to prevent the dust problem. Wooden treads are usually carpeted since they will wear appreciably over the years. If you visit spirited houses or read magazines and books featuring them, you will get other ideas for stair-tread material. Avoid prefabricated frame stairs with pressed-board treads. If they are what your budget dictates, cover the treads with carpet and dress them up with rustic railings of natural materials.

Railings offer great opportunity for creativity. The classic rail in a log home—found on stairs, lofts, and porches—has newels, rails, and balusters of straight, hand-peeled logs four to six inches in diameter fit together in a mortise-and-tenon fashion. These are attractive and serviceable giving a sense of strength and substance. The most interesting rail systems are made of twisting branches or twigs, often woven together to fill the space between the curving upper and lower rails. Many

*A spiral staircase
can be a dramatic
and useful element
in a small kitchen.*

examples of these creative, handcrafted railings can be found in old lodges and in the buildings of the national parks.

Most of these rails could not be built today. The National Building Code requires that railings on stairs, lofts, and balconies be constructed so that a four-inch sphere cannot pass through. To meet this requirement, twig railing systems would have to be tightly fit with no gaps larger than the specification, or they would have to be backed by mesh such as chicken wire or a solid surface such as tempered glass or rigid plastic. This is a challenge for the craftsman, but when well executed, it creates a centerpiece rail system.

Railings don't have to be built of log or twig. Many alpine homes have traditionally had rough-sawn plank balusters carefully shaped with cutouts that represent the area or the family living in the home. These planks, evenly spaced, can make up all of the vertical elements of the balustrade or can be combined with log or square-cut balusters to open them up.

Staircases often end on a large landing or loft that strengthens the open feeling begun on the ground level. The center section of a U-shaped staircase can be a broad, flat walkway with room for a bookcase and reading chair. It can also be an exciting place for a sweeping window seat. Landings can be areas that overlook the lodge room, adding another visual level to the room dimensions. A loft under a low ceiling can be a sitting area, home office, or extra sleeping space. Perhaps the richest-looking loft is that used as a library. Lofts do not have to be an entire staircase above the main floor. A loft opening midway up the run of stairs adds to the flow of the floor plan and creates another eye-catching level.

By incorporating elements resembling pine branches and pinecones, this staircase creates a unique natural space.

Stonework

Rock has long been the natural element used for strength and solidity. For parts of the home that come in contact with fire or moisture, stone is a good choice. Wherever it is used, stone is dramatic.

Traditionally, stone was dug from creeks, streams, and riverbanks, picked up from fields, or hauled from mountain- and hillsides near the building site. Today, it is bought from stone yards and quarries, and you may or may not be able to match the stone that resides on your property. For example, the supply of granite mossrock available for building has been almost exhausted. If it can't be matched, look for an alternative that blends in both shape and color.

Since not much natural rock is currently produced, a viable alternative to natural rock is cultured stone. This man-made product is so well done, it will fool the eye. It is a cost-effective way to go, though most of the cultured material, made of cement, is no less weighty than the real thing.

Stone is sold by the ton and will cover varying surface areas, depending on the type of stone.

For instance, the ton of flagstone you buy for a walkway could cover about 125 square feet, while the ton of irregular depth-stone veneer for facing the fireplace and applying around the foundation might only cover 45 square feet.

Stonemasons can charge by the job or by the square foot. Either way, stonework is labor-intensive and therefore expensive. Plan on installation

Stone, masterfully fitted, adds a rustic atmosphere when used in small doses or large, such as in this rugged wall.

of stone to add somewhere in the neighborhood of $15 per square foot.

Stonework should have an irregular pattern and the look of being hand laid not by a master stonemason but by a weekend woodsman. No matter what stone is used, harsh straight lines cannot produce this. Many lines need to be straight for the structure, but soften them by varying the projection of individual stones. Rugged profiles and sweeping lines are a hallmark of this construction.

Rock can be put to use in infinite ways. Local rock on early-twentieth-century camps and lodges rooted them to the setting, making them look as though they sprouted there. Used with taste and restraint, stone not only blends the home into its surroundings but adds great interest. If your land has abundant rock, you may have a ready supply. If you must purchase stone and are alarmed by flashing dollar signs, remember that a few simple touches work wonders.

Landscape

As landscape material, rock stands alone, is dry stacked, or is set in mortar. Begin utilizing it where one drives onto the property. That first glimpse could be as uncomplicated as a large boulder set into the ground. Affix rustic iron address numbers to

A rock walkway winds its way to the front door of a home whose lower walls and pediments are sheathed in stone.

the boulder, plant low-growing evergreens around it and perhaps a few wildflowers or other favorites to bloom throughout the growing season. A stone pillar can hold an iron lamppost with a hanging lantern and address numbers. Broaden the pillar to hold the mailbox. This will introduce visitors with style.

Beyond the entry, stone landscape elements tame slopes, line planting beds, and make easy-care curved walkways and steps leading to the home. A stone bench added to your favorite area of the yard makes an at-home getaway. If rock, budget, and/or muscle survive the building project, add a stone patio and barbecue.

Exterior Stone

When it comes to house building, stone can form the walls themselves, but it is generally applied to concrete or frame walls that provide the necessary support not only for the structure but for the rock. While this allows the builder to insulate the structural wall, building against a straight wall makes it more difficult to obtain the weighty, monolithic look of those old lodge walls. Once again, strive to apply rock in an irregular manner—size, shape, and profile—avoiding flat surfaces and sharp lines.

If used as infill on a log or timber frame, the stone must still be built against a frame wall, even though infill is not

A stone pillar and a handcrafted lantern light the homecoming for residents and their guests.

required to be structural. All walls must meet R-factor requirements, and when those walls are stone, that requires insulation.

Stone is a logical choice for chimneys. When appropriate, give them a graceful sweep, and a massive profile. Consider including a formation of numbers to proclaim the year of construction in the rockwork of the chimney.

Substantial stone pillars can also support porches, decks, breezeways, and pergolas.

Interior Stone

Pull touches of the exterior stone inside to give the project unity. The ruggedness of a stone-paved floor is an added benefit to its natural beauty. Use stone wherever moisture might be present—foyer, dining room, bath, and kitchen— and warm it up with radiant-floor heating.

Stone can be a functioning kick-wall at the breakfast bar or a natural lining for a shower. Use a stone wall as a backdrop for an indoor waterfall. Small or large, consider one in the entry, as a half-wall partition between the dining room and lodge room, or make it useful as well as dramatic in a large shower.

Nothing heralds warmth and welcome like a crackling fire in a big stone fireplace. In many areas, you will find you can't build that dream fireplace anymore. Building codes specify fireplaces must be either prefabricated or fitted with an insert built to pass Environmental Protection Agency regulations. They also require fitting with a catalytic converter to reduce smoke and particulate emissions to acceptable levels. To solve this, fireplace inserts are primarily used in existing construction. To use an insert in

Setting a wood stove into a stone surround can give it the scale needed to balance with the mass of a log building.

new construction, you must first build an expensive masonry fireplace, then fill it with a black metal box and cover the beautiful stone front with a sheet of iron fitted with a door. Few people go this route on a new fireplace since building with a prefab unit can give you an almost identical effect for less money. Prefab models currently on the market that satisfy EPA standards are small—and look minuscule when placed in a room of large scale and proportion. The few larger prefabs available that meet specifications are pricey, though there is the hope that complaints from log home builders will soon broaden the market and lower the cost.

Don't resolve yourself to building a flat, tall, boxy chimney. With a little imagination you can come up with a comfortable solution. One way is to install a large EPA-approved wood-burning stove in a stone surround. The firebox combined with the darkened cave of the surround can give the impression of a much larger fireplace, and a generous hearth, a deep mantel, and an arch of raised stone can provide depth and mass.

The flagstone that paves the floor also covers the fireplace. Fieldstone pillars add texture and interest.

A second option is to set the fireplace in an attention-grabbing architectural element. A rustic inglenook or alcove can step your attention down to a smaller space before it focuses on the fireplace. This creates a delightful, cozy sitting area that you might never have thought to build. Be careful to check the specifications of the chosen fire unit. Some manufacturers, especially of wood-burning stoves, have regulations concerning installation in anything that could be considered an alcove.

Since wood-burning regulations are only bound to get tighter, it might be wise to look into gas log fireplace and stove units; most are quite handsome. In addition, stove units have the added benefit of being capable of serving as the main heat source for the home, replacing basement furnaces with attractive firelight. They can be vented directly without need of an expensive chimney and require less clearance from combustibles.

Whatever you choose for the fireplace or stove, craft it generously. Play the verticality of its chimney against horizontal elements such as lofts or stair landings. Grant your fireplace the premier spot in the home. After all, it's at the heart of this architectural genre.

Nooks and Crannies

Nooks and crannies tend to be the places that are left over when other features are built—the areas under the stairs, the corners of lofts, places without stand-up-headroom. They break up square rooms and add interest to wall and floor expanses. Nooks and crannies can also become favorite places.

One functional nook is a window seat. It can be a space as small as three or four feet wide and two feet deep where you can stop during the day for a cup of tea and thought-gathering. It can also be a larger space, fitted with a twin-bed mattress and lined with layers of pillows. Window seats encourage quiet activities like reading, writing, or catching up on homework. Equip yours with good overhead lighting. Use the area under the seat for a deep drawer or two to stow board games, linens, or photo albums.

Window seats may be built in one of two ways. The first is nonstructural and could easily be added to an existing structure. Build out into the room with a supporting structure on either side of the window. This could be done with a simple wall but would look better if framed with floor-to-ceiling closets, cabinets, or shelves above lower cabinets. Build the window seat under the window and between the cabinets. Pad the bench and build drawers beneath it.

A balcony tucked under a low roof makes an all-weather spot to enjoy the view of the lake beyond.

© 1995 Roger Wade

Areas with low ceilings can be used for many activities. The space here, when furnished with a log desk and chair, becomes a peaceful writing niche.

The second way is structural and will need to be properly designed. In this method, the window seat is built into a bay window that protrudes from the exterior wall. It has the advantage of having windows in the sides of the bay, making light and outside view available from three sides. It must be supported from below either by a foundation or bracing against the exterior wall on which it is built. It must also be covered by its own roof.

The space under the stairs is an ideal nook. Often it is used for storage, but it could be designed as valuable activity area. For instance, it may be just the place for a small home office. Build in a desk, add some good lighting, and fit filing cabinets into the area under the lower steps.

If you have teenagers, consider outfitting the area under the stairs as a phone booth. Fill the floor with pillows or add a comfortable chair. Wire in a light or lamp and hang a chalk and bulletin board for messages and reminders. Add some shelves—for phone books, pencils, paper, and homework—and a door.

That same space could be a playhouse, clubhouse, or fort for younger children. Line the walls with cork, and a simple change of pictures can transform it from a grocery store to a fast-food drive-in. Consider giving it a Dutch door.

The place under the loft is another area for a special treatment. Add two overstuffed chairs to create an intimate spot for quiet conversation. If that area is in the lodge room, build in a plush, three-sided banquette with a table fitted in the U. It can be used for dinners by the fire, games and craft projects, or working on the laptop.

Built-in bunks stand ever ready to provide a comfortable night's sleep. The drawers built into the mattress platform are a great use of space.

A large dormer makes a snug recess for a bed,
appropriately covered with a log-cabin quilt.

The dormers that admit light into the second story also make attractive alcoves that extend the outline of the room and provide usable spaces. Depending on their size, they could hold a desk, built-in storage, plants, or a small television and a coffeemaker. Larger areas could hold a piano, a train table, or a trundle bed. Even larger alcoves can house sitting areas, fireplaces, or a table and chairs. A sitting room off the master bedroom is a flexible space that can double as a nursery, sewing room, office, or retreat.

The most nook-and-cranny square footage can be had along the knee wall of an upper story. A knee wall is one shorter than full height. Because of its construction, it automatically lacks the necessary headroom for one to stand up in, so is often left idle. This can be made into a better-functioning space by outfitting it to become a craft or work space. Use some of it for easy-to-reach storage by building in drawers and cabinets. If the space is in a child's room or playroom, wall off a portion of it for a playhouse. Give the door a cabin look, add a plastic window, and it will be outfitted for generations of little ones. Areas on either side can hold drawers or cabinets for games, toys, and out-of-season clothing.

Nooks and crannies are sure to become favorite places and focal points for your home, even if they look as though they happened by accident.

© 1995 Roger Wade

Window seats flank the fireplace, offering quiet lounging for one and extra seating for a crowd.

Special Effects

In general, people who build rustic homes are very involved in the design and building, and, as a result, the builder's thoughts and designs can be reflected in special effects.

Many of those effects are thought of as finishing details, such as floor, wall, and ceiling coverings. Normally these would be the last decisions, but since spirited buildings don't always use standard materials, many architectural dimensions will depend on the manner in which the surrounding areas are finished. You will save yourself and your builder lots of aggravation if you decide on any nonstandard finishes early on and draw up the plans with these in mind.

For example, flooring depth can change the height of the first step of the staircase. If you are using recycled flooring, wood from a lumber mill, stone, or any number of floors, they will likely be deeper than the standard tile, prefinished hardwood flooring, or carpet that most homes are treated to. If you build the stairs without taking the flooring depth into consideration, you may end up with the first step being much shorter than the others. Building code requires a limited height variance within the run of a staircase. If you decide ahead of time on that flooring, the staircase can be adjusted to accommodate it in the plans, or at least at the time the stairs are built. If the treads on your staircase will be thicker than normal, it's also helpful to have that on the plans.

Carved posts, such as this alert hare, should be finished well before the time for installation.

Cypress logs sliced into rounds were set into mortar and finished. Countless hours of labor created this masterpiece.

© 2000 Rocky Mountain Log Homes

© 2000 Rocky Mountain Log Homes

Many people install in-floor radiant heat these days for its quiet, uniform warmth. If wanted, space needs to be allowed. Changing the floor thickness can affect door-frame and counter heights as well as step height.

Artistically carved posts can enhance the theme of your home and should be carved before installation. Carved supporting posts need to be installed very early in the construction process. Carvings should be used sparingly. Make sure they do not to compromise the log's load-bearing capacity.

If you are using hand-crafted doors or any doors larger than the standard, decide early and make sure the dimension is built into the floor plan when adjustments can easily be made.

Many people like their kitchen counters a few inches taller than the average. But when you top them with thicker counters and a backsplash, they can rise into the window area. While most backsplashes can be cut to fit around the window, ordering a different-sized window is a neater solution.

With a bit of forethought, a receding arched panel can be built to display a trophy elk or prized artwork. Without the niche, the fireplace façade would lack depth and interest.

Beginning

Whether adding rustic details to an existing dwelling, building a new house from a stock plan or a kit, or constructing a home of your own design, the time will come when the study and idea gathering are behind you and it is time to begin. Planning a dream home is exciting . . . and daunting, but by applying the details in this book, you can be assured your home will have a unique and satisfying character.

Keep in mind that your home does not have to look like any you see in books or magazines. It is yours and has only to satisfy your tastes and lifestyle, your budget, and your building department.

Budget will dictate many choices. When you cannot afford the ideal, don't look at it as settling for something less. View it as an opportunity to explore options and find creative solutions. It is that creativity that will give your home individuality.

As you design and prepare to build, remember, the journey is as important as the destination. Be involved. Work only with people who will add their own energy and integrity to the project. Under the best of circumstances, the journey will have stressful moments. Strive to keep the building process in its proper place. After all is said, done, and built, it is not the walls, the roof system, the doors and windows that are of prime importance. They are a backdrop for the living that will go on within. May yours be spirited!

*Design need not
be complicated
to be inspired.*

*Spirited homes are
one-of-a-kind shelters
that reflect their
builders' personalities.*

© 1999 Brad Simmons

© 1999 Brad Simmons

*Mixed materials
crafted with thought
and style can help the
budget and add an
air of individuality.*

Architects and Draftsmen

Babcock Design Group
52 Exchange Place
Salt Lake City, UT 84111
801-531-1144

Concept Design Inst.
310 Grand Ave.
Laramie, WY 82070
307-721-5907
Custom blueprints for log, timber-frame,
stone, and other buildings

Phil Haas, Log Home Designer
7570 N. Foothills Hwy.
Boulder, CO 80302
Haashaus@USWest.net
Custom house designs, log frame and log

Logmaker
3D Log Home Design CAD software
www.logmaker.com

Morter Aker Architects
143 East Meadow Drive
Vail, CO 81657
970-476-5105

Kal-log
On-line consultation and advice
on building with logs
www.kal-log.com

Robertson Miller Terrell Architects
P.O. Box 7630
Avon, CO 81620
970-949-0916
RMT@vail.net

Builders

You'll find lists of more log-home builders in log-home magazines, in your local phone book, and on the Internet.

Foothills Log Homes
Curt Dirkes
13050 N. Foothills Hwy.
Longmont, CO 80503
303-823-9058
fax 303-727-6764

Garland Homes
2172 Hwy. 93 N.
Victor, MT 59875
406-642-3095
www.garlandhomes.com

Honka Homes U.S.A.
P.O. Box 3398
Evergreen, CO 80439
877-US-Honka
www.honka.com
info@honka.com

Log Knowledge
P.O. Box 1025
Laporte, CO 80535
970-493-1973

Rocky Mountain Log Homes
1883 Hwy. 93 S.
Hamilton, MT 59840
406-363-5680
www.rmlh.com

Logs, Slabs, Siding

Look under lumber mills, sawmills, lumber, log home, buildings, and cabins and lumber wholesale in your phone book for possible dealers in your area.

Alpine Log Mill
2640 South 1500 East
Vernal, UT 84078
435-781-2651
www.webstorage.com/~houlton/a/alpine1.htm
House logs, chinking, and finishing supplies

Cedar Craft Log Homes, Inc.
ph/fax 517-236-7395
Hand-peeled half-log siding, hand-hewn timbers

Hester's Log and Lumber
231 West Eagle Nest Trail
Kremmling, CO 80459
970-724-3868
Peeled or unpeeled log and log slabs, etc.

K & K Lumber & Log Sales
286 Harness Lane
(P.O. Box 210)
Silt, CO 81652
970-876-2156
kklumber@rof.net
Round peeled or unpeeled logs, D-shape
tongue & groove house logs, log siding
to match house logs, custom-cut beams

Logsiding.com
Plans, design and drafting service,
siding, paneling, supplies
www.logsiding.com

Meadow Valley Log Siding
800-657-4666
www.mvloghomes.com
Mill-direct log siding

Satterwhite Log Homes
800-777-7288
Dead-standing Engleman spruce
tongue-and-groove house logs

Shaughnessy Forest Products
P. O. Box 1057
Campton, NH 03223
603-726-4548
www.shaughnessy.net
shaughnessy@cyberportal.net
Hardwood logs, softwood logs, veneer logs

Timberfab. Inc.
1-800-968-8322
www.tfab.com
tfab@coastalnet.com
Timber-framed roof systems, timber
frames, log-home supplies

Fireplaces and Stoves

Friendly Fire, Inc.
1802 LaPorte Ave.
Ft. Collins, CO 80524
970-484-8593

Post and Rails

Custom Log Furniture and Design
19351 Hwy. 82
Carbondale, CO 81623
970-963-4181
custom@sopris.net

Geronimo Pole Co.
530-265-2836
Hand-peeled poles and timbers—
rafters, railings, mantels, and more

Posts and Rails
888-745-8965
www.postsandrails.com

Precision Pine, Inc.
8919 Valgro Rd.
Knoxville, TN 37920
423-573-5322

StairMeister Log Works
5854 Rawhide Ct. Ste. A
Boulder, CO 80302
303-440-2994
fax 303-440-0736

TJ's Wood Products
P. O. Box 437
Bailey, CO 80421
800-530-0275 or 303 838-5779
www.tjswood.com

Building Supplies

Schroeder Log Home Supply, Inc.
800-359-6614
218-326-4434
fax 218-326-2529
www.loghelp.com

Organiclear
Wood coatings, finishes, and sealers
800-825-7650
www.standardtar.com
standtar@aol.com

Log Finishers' Supply
545 Turner Drive
Durango, CO 81301
888-840-8445

Rocky Mountain Hardware
888-788-2013
fax 208-788-2577
www.rockymountainhardware.com

Furnishings

Rocky Mountain Home Collection
Vicki Stroud
128 S. College Ave.
Ft. Collins, CO 80524
970-482-8608
Furniture, quilts, artwork, and lighting

The Painted Moose
3591 Cocanougher Lane
Perryville, KY 40468
606-332-7500
moose@bradsimmons.com
Lodge, cabin, and cowboy home furnishings
and accessories